GOING ON A
PILGRIMAGE

Written by
Christine H. Huynh, M.D.

Illustrated by
Elsie S. Barcena

Dharma Wisdom, LLC

Going on a Pilgrimage
Bringing the Buddha's Teachings into Practice series
Copyright 2021 by Dharma Wisdom, LLC

Dharma Wisdom, LLC
Arlington, Texas
dharmawisdomdw@gmail.com

Author: Christine H. Huynh, M.D.
Illustrator: Elsie Barcena

Library of Congress Control Number: 2021921559

ISBN: 978-1-951175-05-4

First Edition 2021

I went on a pilgrimage to visit the four important sites of the Buddha's life. These holy sites mark the extraordinary events of his birth, Enlightenment (Awakening), First Sermon, and Nirvana. This was my first trip to India and Nepal!

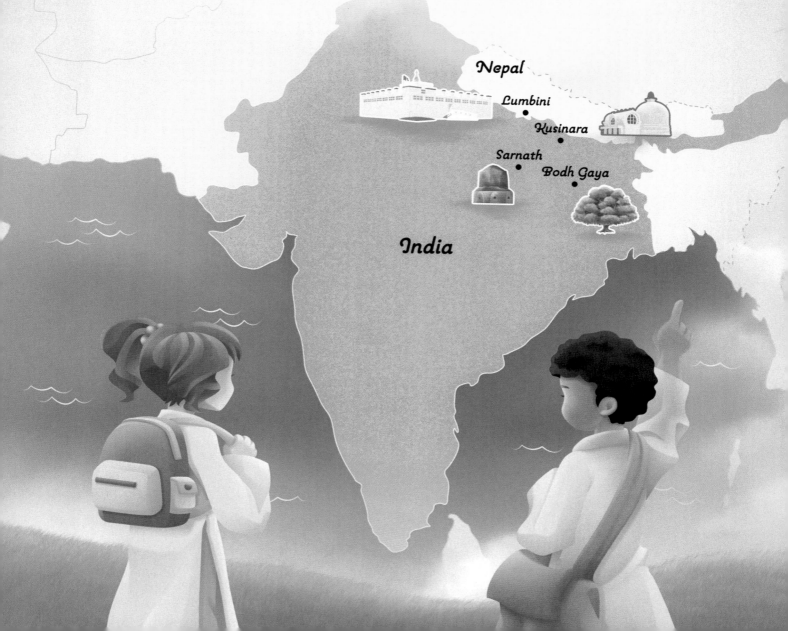

Nepal

Lumbini

Kusinara

Sarnath

Bodh Gaya

India

Lumbini garden was where the Buddha's mother, Queen Maya, rested while traveling to her parents' home to give birth. It is in Nepal, just north of India. Here, the Buddha came into the world unexpectedly while Queen Maya was holding onto an Ashoka tree (Ashoka means "without sorrow" in Sanskrit).

Bodh Gaya, India was where the Buddha attained Awakening under the Bodhi Tree. It is actually a pippala tree (a sacred fig tree), but was so named because it is the tree where Prince Siddhartha attained awakening. This broad tree provided a cool shade and a peaceful place for him to achieve Enlightenment. Oooh... this was when the Buddha saw and understood everything in the world.

The Buddha gave his first teaching to his five friends at Deer Park in Sarnath. His Dharma teaching is a precious Jewel! This was when the Three Jewels (the Buddha, the Dharma, and the Sangha) were formed.

The Buddha passed away peacefully between two solid Sal trees in Kusinara. His passing is called Nirvana - which also means true, inner joy or the elimination of the negatives. Even though he is not with us anymore, the good things he has done will always be remembered.

Oh, what a delight it was to be walking on the land that the Buddha walked. I felt much joy and peace as this experience deeply touched my heart. It is a blessing to be able to see, hear, feel, and witness these four sacred places.

Lumbini

Sarnath

Kusinara

Bodh Gaya

A pilgrimage is a journey to experience spiritual growth. It was not anything like a fancy vacation. I walked on dirt roads, rode on rickshaws, and saw people being carried by two men because they could not walk the long distance.

I learned to be flexible and adapt to the bumpy roads on the bus trips to distant sites. I waited for rest stops to buy snacks to eat and go to restrooms.

There were no conveniences such as nice toilets for me to sit on or Wi-Fi signal for my phone.

I had to be patient and stand in line to go to the porta potty toilet. I had to tolerate not being able to text my friends on my phone.

I accepted the roaming cows along the walkways and the dirt blown in my face. I let go of my uneasy feelings, and I remembered to be happy in the present moment.

I learned not to expect to have pizza or chicken nuggets for meals. Instead, I was very thankful to have food to eat. I ate vegetarian curry every day and was grateful that I had nourishment for my body without causing harm to animals.

I shared my food and money with the kids in remote India because they did not have much. However, it was clear that they had a lot of love and fun outdoors.

It did not matter that I was in an unfamiliar place.
I had a great practice during my pilgrimage.

I practiced being flexible and patient. I practiced acceptance and letting
go. I learned to be thankful for what I have and to not expect more.

I do not have to travel very far to go on a pilgrimage because my life is already a pilgrimage. Any of the activities in my daily life can be my next pilgrimage.

We are flowers that can bring fragrance to one another in our pilgrimage. This fragrance is the joy, love, and comfort that we can give each other. A pilgrimage is an act where I create fragrance for everyone in any situation.

There are several ways that
I can give my fragrance.

I practice to be flexible and adapt to the teacher's
rules instead of doing things my way. I raise my
hand when I want to talk or go to the restroom.
My actions really please my teachers.

I practice being patient so that my friends will not feel hurried.

My friends take such a long time to get dressed, but I would wait without getting upset.

I accept and do things even when I do not like them. I had to take off my shoes at the big holy sites on the pilgrimage. I let go of the uncomfortable feelings of dirt on my bare feet, and I did not make a big fuss so that I can keep peace with my parents and others.

I show gratitude instead of expecting certain things. There are no hamburgers served at the temple! But I see many mothers busy cooking vegetarian foods. I am thankful to have a yummy home-cooked meal.

All these actions are my practice and I do them without complaining or being impatient. My actions make my family and friends very happy. My mindful speech and actions give me a beautiful, bright glow!

Finally we can have fun after cleaning the house!

This is such a nice day to be with my friends.

No running

Being flexible, patient, and accepting does not mean that I give up on a situation. This practice allows me to reflect on the conditions in the present moment. I can then respond with mindfulness in order to create a good outcome. This way, I avoid the habit of reacting on impulse that will result in problems.

This is how I leave a lasting memory in my friends' hearts. They will for sure invite and welcome me to their next fun event.

There are four other important activities that I should perform on my pilgrimage.

The first is to give with an open heart. I can give things that I have - like money, food, or clothing.

I do not need to have a lot in order to give, though. I can donate my hair to make wigs for cancer patients.

A more personal way to give is to offer my happy smile or just to be present for my friends when they need me.

The fourth act is to provide services together with my family
and friends in order to achieve a set goal. We are stronger
as a group than as individuals. Each of our small
good acts will add up to greater good acts.

From my pilgrimage, I can deliver five fragrances to the world:
1) the teachings on morality, 2) my focused attention to do good,
3) the wisdom to act skillfully, 4) freedom for my spirit, and
5) freedom from clinging to my point of view.

My pilgrimage brings the fragrance of good intentions with a calm, clear mind. It helps me to be free from habitual reactions when my emotions are stirred. It shows me how to create joy for myself and others. I am as beautiful as a flower when I release this fragrance.

From this journey, my mind radiates four great qualities that are born from my actions for others:
1) loving-kindness, 2) compassion, 3) joy, and 4) forgiveness. These merits are so huge that they cannot be measured.

LOVING-KINDNESS

JOY

COMPASSION

FORGIVENESS

Loving-kindness makes others cheerful. Compassion relieves suffering in others. Joy is a true, inner happiness. Forgiveness creates mental peace by helping me let go of partial views and not allowing them to bind me.

I vow to create my fragrances wherever I go and to whomever I meet. I will perform actions that can give me the experience of the ultimate life pilgrimage.

Made in the USA
Middletown, DE
07 September 2023

38165998R00020